RECIPE
JOURNAL
My Kitchen Companion

PETER PAUPER PRESS, INC.
WHITE PLAINS, NEW YORK

PETER PAUPER PRESS
Fine Books and Gifts Since 1928

Our Company

In 1928, at the age of twenty-two, Peter Beilenson began printing books on a small press in the basement of his parents' home in Larchmont, New York. Peter—and later his wife, Edna—sought to create fine books that sold at "prices even a pauper could afford."

Today, still family owned and operated, Peter Pauper Press continues to honor our founders' legacy—and our customers' expectations—of beauty, quality, and value.

Copyright © 2012
Peter Pauper Press, Inc.
202 Mamaroneck Avenue
White Plains, NY 10601
All rights reserved
ISBN 978-1-4413-0983-9
Printed in Hong Kong
7 6 5 4 3 2 1

Visit us at www.peterpauper.com

CONTENTS

FOOD FOR THOUGHT

INTRODUCTION

Now you're cooking!

Use this handy organizer to write down the best of tested and tasted creations from your kitchen. It's also the perfect place to record the recipes that mean the most to you, such as heirloom recipes from parents and grandparents. The pocket provided in the back is just the right place to keep other recipes from friends, cooking classes, the Internet, magazines, etc., until you get a chance to write them down. Convenient write-in contents pages for each category enable you to locate recipes in a flash. You'll also find tips, reference charts, and helpful hints that might make it a little easier to whip up that next culinary masterpiece.

Bon appétit!

Approach love and cooking with reckless abandon.

H. JACKSON BROWN, JR.

HELPFUL INFORMATION

MEASUREMENT EQUIVALENTS

LIQUID MEASURES	FLUID OUNCES	METRIC
1 teaspoon	0.16	5 ml
1 tablespoon = 3 teaspoons	0.5	15 ml
1 ounce	1.0	30 ml
1/4 cup = 4 tablespoons	2.0	59 ml
1/3 cup = 5 tablespoons + 1 teaspoon	2.7	79 ml
1/2 cup = 8 tablespoons	4.0	118 ml
1 cup = 16 tablespoons	8.0	237 ml
2 cups = 1 pint	16.0	473 ml
4 cups = 1 quart	32.0	946 ml
4-1/4 cups	33.8	1 liter
4 quarts = 16 cups = 1 gallon	128.0	3.78 liter

DRY MEASURES	OUNCES BY WEIGHT	METRIC
3 teaspoons = 1 tablespoon	0.5	14.3 grams
2 tablespoons = 1/8 cup	1.0	28.35 grams
4 tablespoons = 1/4 cup	2.0	56.7 grams
8 tablespoons = 1/2 cup	4.0	113.4 grams
12 tablespoons = 3/4 cup	6.0	170 grams
16 tablespoons = 1 cup = ½ pound	8.0	226.8 grams
32 tablespoons = 2 cups = 1 pound	16.0	453.6 grams

American standard measures, approximate measurement equivalents

TEMPERATURE EQUIVALENTS

FAHRENHEIT	CELSIUS	GAS MARK (U.K.)
250°	120°	1/2
275°	135°	1
300°	150°	2
325°	165°	3
350°	180°	4
375°	190°	5
400°	200°	6
425°	220°	7
450°	230°	8
475°	245°	9

Approximate equivalents

STORAGE & FREEZER TIPS

- Keep refrigerator temperature between 34° F (1 C°) and 40° F (4 C°). Keep freezer temperature at 0° F (-17° C).
- Always thaw frozen foods in the refrigerator or microwave. Follow manufacturer's instructions for microwave thawing of foods. Thawing food at room temperature promotes bacterial growth.
- Never refreeze food that has been thawed.
- Keep uncooked meat, poultry, and fish in the coldest part of the refrigerator. Use within 1-2 days, or freeze.
- Do not wash fresh fruits and vegetables before storing them in the refrigerator. Store loosely to allow air to circulate. Wash thoroughly immediately before using.
- Many dry foods such as ground coffee, spices, and flour will stay fresher if refrigerated in an air-tight container.
- Except for ice cream, dairy products do not freeze well.
- Never freeze eggs in the shell—they will burst.

COOKING HINTS

- When measuring ingredients, level off dry measures with the flat blade of a knife. Measure liquids on a level surface.

- Flour increases in volume after sifting, so measure before sifting.

- A little lemon juice will prevent produce such as avocados and apples from turning brown.

- A meat thermometer will help ensure properly cooked meats.

- Do onions make you cry? Try refrigerating them until just before use.

USING THE MICROWAVE

- Never use metal containers or utensils in the microwave.

- Avoid cooking foods with high fat content in the microwave.

- When cooking in the microwave, turn or stir foods halfway through the cooking time to ensure even cooking throughout.

- Small, uniform-sized pieces of food will cook more quickly and evenly than large or irregularly-shaped pieces.

- Covering food while cooking or reheating helps retain moisture.

HEALTHIER EATING

- Try substituting olive oil for butter with your bread.
- Experiment with different types of lettuce. Leaf lettuce and spinach contain more nutrients than iceberg lettuce.
- Choose fresh vegetables over frozen, frozen over canned.
- Stir-frying, grilling, and steaming bring out the flavor in vegetables. Add zest with fresh herbs.
- Canned foods often contain added salt. If using in recipes, reduce salt accordingly.

COMPATIBLE HERBS & SPICES FOR SAVORY DISHES

- Beef: basil, bay, coriander/coriander seeds, cumin, dill, marjoram, sage, tarragon, thyme
- Fish: anise, basil, caraway, chives, dill, fennel, lemon balm, parsley, rosemary, sage, tarragon, thyme
- Lamb: bay, caraway, coriander/coriander seeds, cumin, dill, marjoram, mint, sage, rosemary, thyme
- Pork: anise, basil, chervil, coriander/coriander seeds, dill, cumin, fennel, lemon balm, mint, marjoram, rosemary, sage, tarragon, thyme
- Poultry: basil, bay, caraway, coriander/coriander seeds, cumin, dill, lemon balm, mint, parsley, sage, rosemary, tarragon, thyme

WINE PAIRINGS

- Rule of thumb: Serve light wines with light foods and heavy wines with heavy foods.

- Meats, cheeses, other fatty, protein-rich foods: Cabernet Sauvignon, red Bordeaux

- Salty foods and less sweet desserts: sweet Rieslings, white Zinfandel, dessert wines

- Salty, oily, or fatty foods: dry Rieslings, Chablis, Sauvignon Blanc

GLOSSARY OF COOKING TERMS

al dente: slightly undercooked (referring to pasta)

bain-marie: a large, shallow pan of warm water, holding a container of food, which is thus surrounded with gentle heat. This technique is designed to cook delicate dishes slowly and gently without breaking or curdling them. It can also be used to keep cooked foods warm.

baste: to moisten meat or fish with fat or liquid during cooking, to prevent drying out

blanch: to immerse vegetables or meat in boiling water for a few moments

braise: to cook food slowly in a covered pan over low heat with a small amount of liquid

brine: to immerse, preserve, or pickle in salt water (and sometimes additional sweeteners or herbs)

crudités: raw seasonal vegetables, frequently accompanied by a dipping sauce, often served as an appetizer

cube: to cut food into small, evenly sized cubes

cut in: to blend fat and flour together with a pastry blender, or two knives, until the mixture forms coarse crumbs of uniform size

dash: a very small amount, less than 1/8 teaspoon

dice: to cut food into very small cubes (1/4 inch)

dot: to place small bits of butter, etc., on top of pastry or other dishes

dredge: to coat thoroughly, as with flour

fillet (filet): 1. a piece of poultry, meat, or fish from which the bones have been removed 2. to cut the bones from a piece of meat or fish

fines herbes: a mixture of herbs such as parsley, chervil, chives, and tarragon used as a seasoning.

flute: to make decorative indentations, as on the edge of a piecrust

fold: to blend delicate ingredients such as whipped cream or beaten egg whites gently into a heavier mixture

gratin: a dish topped with bread crumbs or cheese mixed with bits of butter, then heated under the broiler or in the oven until crisp and brown

julienne: to slice into thin strips about the size of matchsticks

knead: to work dough with a press-and-fold motion

lard: 1. rendered pork fat used in baking 2. to insert long, thin strips of fat (usually pork) or bacon into a dry cut of meat to make the cooked meat more tender and flavorful

marbled: Meat that is marbled shows visible fat throughout, which makes it tenderer.

marinade: a seasoned liquid in which foods such as meat, fish, and vegetables are soaked, or marinated, until they absorb flavor and become tender

meringue: a mixture of stiffly beaten egg whites and sugar

mince: to cut or grind into very tiny pieces

parboil: to boil for a short period of time, until partially cooked

poach: to cook in simmering liquid

purée: to push food through a fine sieve or blend in a food processor until smooth and very thick

sauté: to cook food quickly in a skillet over direct heat using a small amount of oil or fat

scald: to heat liquid to just below the boiling point

score: to make shallow cuts in the surface of certain foods, such as meat or fish

simmer: to cook food in liquid over low heat maintained just below the boiling point

steam: to cook food over boiling water in a covered pan with holes in the bottom to let steam through

truss: to secure poultry with string or skewers so that it holds its shape while cooking

whip: to introduce air into a mixture by beating rapidly with a hand beater, whisk, or electric beater

zest: the aromatic outermost skin layer of citrus fruit. Only the colored portion of the skin is used, as the white pith has a bitter flavor.

EMERGENCY SUBSTITUTIONS

baking powder, double-acting. 1 teaspoon (5 g) = 1 teaspoon (5 g) baking soda plus 1/2 teaspoon (2.5 ml) cream of tartar

brown sugar. 1 cup (200 g) = 1 cup granulated sugar (225 g), 2 tablespoons (30 ml) molasses or treacle

buttermilk. 1 cup (237 ml) = 1 tablespoon (15 ml) lemon juice or vinegar plus enough milk to make 1 cup (237 ml) and let stand five minutes, or use 1 cup (237 ml) yogurt

cake flour or extra-fine plain flour. 1 cup (100 g) = 1 cup (125 g) all-purpose or plain flour minus 2 tablespoons (16 g)

chocolate, semisweet. 1 ounce (28 g) = 1 ounce (28 g) unsweetened chocolate plus 1 tablespoon (14 g) granulated sugar

heavy cream (40% fat content). 1 cup (237 ml) = 2/3 cup (158 ml) milk and 1/3 cup (75.6 g) butter

herbs, fresh. 1 tablespoon (15 g) fresh herbs = 1 teaspoon (5 g) dry herbs

egg. 1 large egg = ¼ cup (59 ml) commercial liquid egg substitute; or 1 egg white and 2 teaspoons (10 ml) oil; or (in baking) 1/2 teaspoon (2.5 g) double-acting baking powder, 1 tablespoon (15 ml) vinegar, and 1 tablespoon (15 ml) liquid (use whatever liquid the recipe calls for)

egg yolk. 1 egg yolk = 2 tablespoons (30 ml) commercial egg substitute

flour, all-purpose or plain. 1 cup (125 g) = 1 cup (125 g) plus 2 tablespoons (12.5 g) cake flour or extra-fine flour

flour, self-rising. 1 cup (125 g) = 1 cup (125 g) all-purpose or plain flour plus 1-1/2 teaspoons (7 g) double-acting baking powder and 1/8 teaspoon (1 dash) salt

honey. 1 cup (340 g) = 3/4 cup (169 g) granulated sugar plus 1/4 cup (59.25 ml) liquid (use whatever liquid the recipe calls for)

milk. 1 cup (237 ml) = 1/2 cup (118.5 ml) evaporated milk plus 1/2 cup (118.5 ml) water; or use dry, powdered milk and mix according to directions

sour cream. 1 cup (237 ml) = 1 cup (237 ml) plain yogurt

sugar, granulated. 1 cup (225 g) = 1 cup (200 g) packed light brown sugar, or 1-3/4 cups (219 g) confectioner's (or icing) sugar

American standard measurements used, approximate equivalents

RECIPES

Keep a record of your recipes throughout this section. Each recipe gets two pages. Write down the recipe source, number of servings/quantity, prep time/cook time, ingredients, directions, and your comments. Every category begins with a fill-in Table of Contents that will help you locate your recipes more easily.

NOTES

BRUNCH

*I have trouble with toast.
Toast is very difficult. You have to
watch it all the time or it burns up.*

JULIA CHILD

RECIPE	PAGE

RECIPE

FROM:

SERVINGS: PREP/COOK TIME:

INGREDIENTS:

NOTES/SUBSTITUTIONS:

DIRECTIONS:

WINE PAIRINGS:

DIFFICULTY:

Easy ☐ Medium ☐ Hard ☐

OVERALL RATING ☆☆☆☆☆

RECIPE

FROM:

SERVINGS:　　　　PREP/COOK TIME:

INGREDIENTS:

NOTES/SUBSTITUTIONS:

DIRECTIONS:

WINE PAIRINGS:

DIFFICULTY:

Easy ☐ Medium ☐ Hard ☐

OVERALL RATING ☆☆☆☆☆

RECIPE

FROM:

SERVINGS: PREP/COOK TIME:

INGREDIENTS:

NOTES/SUBSTITUTIONS:

DIRECTIONS:

WINE PAIRINGS:

DIFFICULTY:

Easy ☐ Medium ☐ Hard ☐

OVERALL RATING ☆☆☆☆☆

RECIPE

FROM:

SERVINGS: PREP/COOK TIME:

INGREDIENTS:

NOTES/SUBSTITUTIONS:

DIRECTIONS:

WINE PAIRINGS:

DIFFICULTY:

Easy ☐ Medium ☐ Hard ☐

OVERALL RATING ☆☆☆☆☆

RECICPE

FROM:

SERVINGS: PREP/COOK TIME:

INGREDIENTS:

NOTES/SUBSTITUTIONS:

DIRECTIONS:

WINE PAIRINGS:

DIFFICULTY:

Easy ☐ Medium ☐ Hard ☐

OVERALL RATING ☆☆☆☆☆

RECIPE

FROM:

SERVINGS: PREP/COOK TIME:

INGREDIENTS:

NOTES/SUBSTITUTIONS:

DIRECTIONS:

WINE PAIRINGS:

DIFFICULTY:

Easy ☐ Medium ☐ Hard ☐

OVERALL RATING ☆☆☆☆☆

RECIPE

FROM:

SERVINGS: PREP/COOK TIME:

INGREDIENTS:

NOTES/SUBSTITUTIONS:

DIRECTIONS:

WINE PAIRINGS:

DIFFICULTY:

Easy ☐ Medium ☐ Hard ☐

OVERALL RATING ☆☆☆☆☆

RECIPE

FROM:

SERVINGS: PREP/COOK TIME:

INGREDIENTS:

NOTES/SUBSTITUTIONS:

DIRECTIONS:

WINE PAIRINGS:

DIFFICULTY:

Easy ☐ Medium ☐ Hard ☐

OVERALL RATING ☆☆☆☆☆

RECIPE

FROM:

SERVINGS: PREP/COOK TIME:

INGREDIENTS:

NOTES/SUBSTITUTIONS:

DIRECTIONS:

WINE PAIRINGS:

DIFFICULTY:

Easy ☐ Medium ☐ Hard ☐

OVERALL RATING ☆☆☆☆☆

RECIPE

FROM:

SERVINGS: PREP/COOK TIME:

INGREDIENTS:

NOTES/SUBSTITUTIONS:

DIRECTIONS:

WINE PAIRINGS:

DIFFICULTY:

Easy ☐ Medium ☐ Hard ☐

OVERALL RATING ☆☆☆☆☆

NOTES

APPETIZERS

*Part of the secret to success
is to eat what you like and let the
food fight it out inside.*

MARK TWAIN

RECIPE	PAGE

RECIPE

FROM:

SERVINGS: PREP/COOK TIME:

INGREDIENTS:

NOTES/SUBSTITUTIONS:

DIRECTIONS:

WINE PAIRINGS:

DIFFICULTY:

Easy ☐ Medium ☐ Hard ☐

OVERALL RATING ☆☆☆☆☆

RECIPE

FROM:

SERVINGS: PREP/COOK TIME:

INGREDIENTS:

NOTES/SUBSTITUTIONS:

DIRECTIONS:

WINE PAIRINGS:

DIFFICULTY:

Easy ☐ Medium ☐ Hard ☐

OVERALL RATING ☆☆☆☆☆

RECIPE

FROM:

SERVINGS: PREP/COOK TIME:

INGREDIENTS:

NOTES/SUBSTITUTIONS:

DIRECTIONS:

WINE PAIRINGS:

DIFFICULTY:

Easy ☐ Medium ☐ Hard ☐

OVERALL RATING ☆☆☆☆☆

RECIPE

FROM:

SERVINGS: PREP/COOK TIME:

INGREDIENTS:

NOTES/SUBSTITUTIONS:

DIRECTIONS:

WINE PAIRINGS:

DIFFICULTY:

Easy ☐ Medium ☐ Hard ☐

OVERALL RATING ☆☆☆☆☆

RECIPE

FROM:

SERVINGS: PREP/COOK TIME:

INGREDIENTS:

NOTES/SUBSTITUTIONS:

DIRECTIONS:

WINE PAIRINGS:

DIFFICULTY:

Easy ☐ Medium ☐ Hard ☐

OVERALL RATING ☆☆☆☆☆

RECIPE

FROM:

SERVINGS: PREP/COOK TIME:

INGREDIENTS:

NOTES/SUBSTITUTIONS:

DIRECTIONS:

WINE PAIRINGS:

DIFFICULTY:

Easy ☐ Medium ☐ Hard ☐

OVERALL RATING ☆☆☆☆☆

RECIPE

FROM:

SERVINGS: PREP/COOK TIME:

INGREDIENTS:

NOTES/SUBSTITUTIONS:

DIRECTIONS:

WINE PAIRINGS:

DIFFICULTY:

Easy ☐ Medium ☐ Hard ☐

OVERALL RATING ☆☆☆☆☆

RECIPE

FROM:

SERVINGS: PREP/COOK TIME:

INGREDIENTS:

NOTES/SUBSTITUTIONS:

DIRECTIONS:

WINE PAIRINGS:

DIFFICULTY:

Easy ☐ Medium ☐ Hard ☐

OVERALL RATING ☆☆☆☆☆

RECIPE

FROM:

SERVINGS: PREP/COOK TIME:

INGREDIENTS:

NOTES/SUBSTITUTIONS:

DIRECTIONS:

WINE PAIRINGS:

DIFFICULTY:

Easy ☐ Medium ☐ Hard ☐

OVERALL RATING ☆☆☆☆☆

RECIPE

FROM:

SERVINGS: PREP/COOK TIME:

INGREDIENTS:

NOTES/SUBSTITUTIONS:

DIRECTIONS:

WINE PAIRINGS:

DIFFICULTY:

Easy ☐ Medium ☐ Hard ☐

OVERALL RATING ☆☆☆☆☆

NOTES

SOUPS, SALADS, & SANDWICHES

Only the pure of heart can make good soup.

LUDWIG VAN BEETHOVEN

RECIPE	PAGE

RECIPE

FROM:

SERVINGS: PREP/COOK TIME:

INGREDIENTS:

NOTES/SUBSTITUTIONS:

DIRECTIONS:

WINE PAIRINGS:

DIFFICULTY:

Easy ☐ Medium ☐ Hard ☐

OVERALL RATING ☆☆☆☆☆

RECEIPE

FROM:

SERVINGS: PREP/COOK TIME:

INGREDIENTS:

NOTES/SUBSTITUTIONS:

DIRECTIONS:

WINE PAIRINGS:

DIFFICULTY:

Easy ☐ Medium ☐ Hard ☐

OVERALL RATING ☆☆☆☆☆

RECIPE

FROM:

SERVINGS: PREP/COOK TIME:

INGREDIENTS:

NOTES/SUBSTITUTIONS:

DIRECTIONS:

WINE PAIRINGS:

DIFFICULTY:

Easy ☐ Medium ☐ Hard ☐

OVERALL RATING ☆☆☆☆☆

RECIPE

FROM:

SERVINGS: PREP/COOK TIME:

INGREDIENTS:

NOTES/SUBSTITUTIONS:

DIRECTIONS:

WINE PAIRINGS:

DIFFICULTY:

Easy ☐ Medium ☐ Hard ☐

OVERALL RATING ☆☆☆☆☆

RECIPE

FROM:

SERVINGS: PREP/COOK TIME:

INGREDIENTS:

NOTES/SUBSTITUTIONS:

DIRECTIONS:

WINE PAIRINGS:

DIFFICULTY:

Easy ☐ Medium ☐ Hard ☐

OVERALL RATING ☆☆☆☆☆

RECeIPE

FROM:

SERVINGS: PREP/COOK TIME:

INGREDIENTS:

NOTES/SUBSTITUTIONS:

DIRECTIONS:

....
....
....
....
....
....
....
....
....
....
....
....
....
....
....
....
....
....
....
....
....
....
....
....
....
....
....
....

WINE PAIRINGS:

DIFFICULTY:

Easy ☐ Medium ☐ Hard ☐

OVERALL RATING ☆☆☆☆☆

RECIPE

FROM:

SERVINGS: PREP/COOK TIME:

INGREDIENTS:

NOTES/SUBSTITUTIONS:

DIRECTIONS:

WINE PAIRINGS:

DIFFICULTY:

Easy ☐ Medium ☐ Hard ☐

OVERALL RATING ☆☆☆☆☆

RECIPE

FROM:

SERVINGS:　　　　　PREP/COOK TIME:

INGREDIENTS:

NOTES/SUBSTITUTIONS:

DIRECTIONS:

WINE PAIRINGS:

DIFFICULTY:

Easy ☐ Medium ☐ Hard ☐

OVERALL RATING ☆☆☆☆☆

RECIPE

FROM:

SERVINGS: | PREP/COOK TIME:

INGREDIENTS:

NOTES/SUBSTITUTIONS:

DIRECTIONS:

WINE PAIRINGS:

DIFFICULTY:

Easy ☐ Medium ☐ Hard ☐

OVERALL RATING ☆☆☆☆☆

RECIPE

FROM:

SERVINGS: PREP/COOK TIME:

INGREDIENTS:

NOTES/SUBSTITUTIONS:

DIRECTIONS:
_____

WINE PAIRINGS:
_____
DIFFICULTY:
Easy ☐ Medium ☐ Hard ☐
OVERALL RATING ☆☆☆☆☆

NOTES

SIDE DISHES

*A good cook is like a sorceress
who dispenses happiness.*

ELSA SCHIAPARELLI

RECIPE	PAGE

RECIPE

FROM:

SERVINGS: PREP/COOK TIME:

INGREDIENTS:

NOTES/SUBSTITUTIONS:

DIRECTIONS:

WINE PAIRINGS:

DIFFICULTY:

Easy ☐ Medium ☐ Hard ☐

OVERALL RATING ☆☆☆☆☆

RECIPE

FROM:

SERVINGS: PREP/COOK TIME:

INGREDIENTS:

NOTES/SUBSTITUTIONS:

DIRECTIONS:

WINE PAIRINGS:

DIFFICULTY:

Easy ☐ Medium ☐ Hard ☐

OVERALL RATING ☆☆☆☆☆

RECIPE

FROM:

SERVINGS: PREP/COOK TIME:

INGREDIENTS:

NOTES/SUBSTITUTIONS:

DIRECTIONS:

_____
_____
_____
_____
_____
_____
_____
_____
_____
_____
_____
_____
_____
_____
_____
_____
_____
_____
_____
_____
_____
_____
_____
_____
_____
_____
_____

WINE PAIRINGS:

DIFFICULTY:

Easy ☐ Medium ☐ Hard ☐

OVERALL RATING ☆☆☆☆☆

RECIPE

FROM:

SERVINGS: PREP/COOK TIME:

INGREDIENTS:

NOTES/SUBSTITUTIONS:

DIRECTIONS:

WINE PAIRINGS:

DIFFICULTY:

Easy ☐ Medium ☐ Hard ☐

OVERALL RATING ☆☆☆☆☆

RECIPE

FROM:

SERVINGS: PREP/COOK TIME:

INGREDIENTS:

NOTES/SUBSTITUTIONS:

DIRECTIONS:

WINE PAIRINGS:

DIFFICULTY:

Easy ☐ Medium ☐ Hard ☐

OVERALL RATING ☆☆☆☆☆

RECIPE

FROM:

SERVINGS: PREP/COOK TIME:

INGREDIENTS:

NOTES/SUBSTITUTIONS:

DIRECTIONS:

WINE PAIRINGS:

DIFFICULTY:

Easy ☐ Medium ☐ Hard ☐

OVERALL RATING ☆☆☆☆☆

RECIPE

FROM:

SERVINGS: PREP/COOK TIME:

INGREDIENTS:

NOTES/SUBSTITUTIONS:

DIRECTIONS:

WINE PAIRINGS:

DIFFICULTY:

Easy ☐ Medium ☐ Hard ☐

OVERALL RATING ☆☆☆☆☆

RECIPE

FROM:

SERVINGS:　　　PREP/COOK TIME:

INGREDIENTS:

NOTES/SUBSTITUTIONS:

DIRECTIONS:

WINE PAIRINGS:

DIFFICULTY:

Easy ☐ Medium ☐ Hard ☐

OVERALL RATING ☆☆☆☆☆

RECIPE

FROM:

SERVINGS: PREP/COOK TIME:

INGREDIENTS:

NOTES/SUBSTITUTIONS:

DIRECTIONS:

WINE PAIRINGS:

DIFFICULTY:

Easy ☐ Medium ☐ Hard ☐

OVERALL RATING ☆☆☆☆☆

RECIPE

FROM:

SERVINGS:　　　　PREP/COOK TIME:

INGREDIENTS:

NOTES/SUBSTITUTIONS:

DIRECTIONS:

WINE PAIRINGS:

DIFFICULTY:

Easy ☐ Medium ☐ Hard ☐

OVERALL RATING ☆☆☆☆☆

NOTES

MAIN COURSES

*The discovery of a new dish
does more for human happiness
than the discovery of a new star.*

JEAN ANTHELME BRILLAT–SAVARIN

RECIPE	PAGE

RECIPE

FROM:

SERVINGS:　　　　PREP/COOK TIME:

INGREDIENTS:

NOTES/SUBSTITUTIONS:

DIRECTIONS:

....

....

....

....

....

....

....

....

....

....

....

....

....

....

....

....

....

....

....

....

....

WINE PAIRINGS:

DIFFICULTY:

Easy ☐ Medium ☐ Hard ☐

OVERALL RATING ☆☆☆☆☆

RECIPE

FROM:

SERVINGS: PREP/COOK TIME:

INGREDIENTS:

NOTES/SUBSTITUTIONS:

DIRECTIONS:

WINE PAIRINGS:

DIFFICULTY:

Easy ☐ Medium ☐ Hard ☐

OVERALL RATING ☆☆☆☆☆

RECIPE

FROM:

SERVINGS: PREP/COOK TIME:

INGREDIENTS:

NOTES/SUBSTITUTIONS:

DIRECTIONS:

_____
_____
_____
_____
_____
_____
_____
_____
_____
_____
_____
_____
_____
_____
_____
_____
_____
_____
_____
_____
_____
_____

WINE PAIRINGS:

DIFFICULTY:

Easy ☐ Medium ☐ Hard ☐

OVERALL RATING ☆☆☆☆☆

RECImPE

FROM:

SERVINGS: PREP/COOK TIME:

INGREDIENTS:

NOTES/SUBSTITUTIONS:

DIRECTIONS:

_____

WINE PAIRINGS:

DIFFICULTY:

Easy ☐ Medium ☐ Hard ☐

OVERALL RATING ☆☆☆☆☆

RECIPE

FROM:

SERVINGS: PREP/COOK TIME:

INGREDIENTS:

NOTES/SUBSTITUTIONS:

DIRECTIONS:

WINE PAIRINGS:

DIFFICULTY:

Easy ☐ Medium ☐ Hard ☐

OVERALL RATING ☆☆☆☆☆

RECIPE

FROM:

SERVINGS:　　　PREP/COOK TIME:

INGREDIENTS:

NOTES/SUBSTITUTIONS:

DIRECTIONS:

WINE PAIRINGS:

DIFFICULTY:

Easy ☐ Medium ☐ Hard ☐

OVERALL RATING ☆☆☆☆☆

RECIPE

FROM:

SERVINGS: PREP/COOK TIME:

INGREDIENTS:

NOTES/SUBSTITUTIONS:

DIRECTIONS:

WINE PAIRINGS:

DIFFICULTY:

Easy ☐ Medium ☐ Hard ☐

OVERALL RATING ☆☆☆☆☆

RECEIPE

FROM:

SERVINGS: PREP/COOK TIME:

INGREDIENTS:

NOTES/SUBSTITUTIONS:

DIRECTIONS:

WINE PAIRINGS:

DIFFICULTY:

Easy ☐ Medium ☐ Hard ☐

OVERALL RATING ☆☆☆☆☆

RECIPE

FROM:

SERVINGS: PREP/COOK TIME:

INGREDIENTS:

NOTES/SUBSTITUTIONS:

DIRECTIONS:

WINE PAIRINGS:

DIFFICULTY:

Easy ☐ Medium ☐ Hard ☐

OVERALL RATING ☆☆☆☆☆

RECIPE

FROM:

SERVINGS: PREP/COOK TIME:

INGREDIENTS:

NOTES/SUBSTITUTIONS:

DIRECTIONS:

WINE PAIRINGS:

DIFFICULTY:

Easy ☐ Medium ☐ Hard ☐

OVERALL RATING ☆☆☆☆☆

NOTES

BREADS & BAKING

The best poet is the man who delivers our daily bread: the local baker.

PABLO NERUDA

RECIPE	PAGE

RECIPE

FROM:

SERVINGS: PREP/COOK TIME:

INGREDIENTS:

NOTES/SUBSTITUTIONS:

DIRECTIONS:

WINE PAIRINGS:

DIFFICULTY:

Easy ☐ Medium ☐ Hard ☐

OVERALL RATING ☆☆☆☆☆

RECITE

FROM:

SERVINGS: PREP/COOK TIME:

INGREDIENTS:

NOTES/SUBSTITUTIONS:

DIRECTIONS:

WINE PAIRINGS:

DIFFICULTY:

Easy ☐ Medium ☐ Hard ☐

OVERALL RATING ☆☆☆☆☆

RECICE

FROM:

SERVINGS: PREP/COOK TIME:

INGREDIENTS:

NOTES/SUBSTITUTIONS:

DIRECTIONS:

_____

_____

_____

_____

_____

_____

_____

_____

_____

_____

_____

_____

_____

_____

_____

_____

_____

_____

WINE PAIRINGS:

DIFFICULTY:

Easy ☐ Medium ☐ Hard ☐

OVERALL RATING ☆☆☆☆☆

RECIPE

FROM:

SERVINGS: PREP/COOK TIME:

INGREDIENTS:

NOTES/SUBSTITUTIONS:

DIRECTIONS:

WINE PAIRINGS:

DIFFICULTY:

Easy ☐ Medium ☐ Hard ☐

OVERALL RATING ☆☆☆☆☆

RECIPE

FROM:

SERVINGS: PREP/COOK TIME:

INGREDIENTS:

NOTES/SUBSTITUTIONS:

DIRECTIONS:

WINE PAIRINGS:

DIFFICULTY:

Easy ☐ Medium ☐ Hard ☐

OVERALL RATING ☆☆☆☆☆

RECIPE

FROM:

SERVINGS: PREP/COOK TIME:

INGREDIENTS:

NOTES/SUBSTITUTIONS:

DIRECTIONS:

WINE PAIRINGS:

DIFFICULTY:

Easy ☐ Medium ☐ Hard ☐

OVERALL RATING ☆☆☆☆☆

RECIPE

FROM:

SERVINGS: PREP/COOK TIME:

INGREDIENTS:

NOTES/SUBSTITUTIONS:

DIRECTIONS:

WINE PAIRINGS:

DIFFICULTY:

Easy ☐ Medium ☐ Hard ☐

OVERALL RATING ☆☆☆☆☆

RECIPE

FROM:

SERVINGS: PREP/COOK TIME:

INGREDIENTS:

NOTES/SUBSTITUTIONS:

DIRECTIONS:

WINE PAIRINGS:

DIFFICULTY:

Easy ☐ Medium ☐ Hard ☐

OVERALL RATING ☆☆☆☆☆

RECIPE

FROM:

SERVINGS: PREP/COOK TIME:

INGREDIENTS:

NOTES/SUBSTITUTIONS:

DIRECTIONS:

_____

_____

_____

_____

_____

_____

_____

_____

_____

_____

_____

_____

_____

_____

_____

_____

_____

_____

_____

_____

_____

_____

_____

WINE PAIRINGS:

DIFFICULTY:

Easy ☐ Medium ☐ Hard ☐

OVERALL RATING ☆☆☆☆☆

RECIPE

FROM:

SERVINGS: PREP/COOK TIME:

INGREDIENTS:

NOTES/SUBSTITUTIONS:

DIRECTIONS:

WINE PAIRINGS:

DIFFICULTY:

Easy ☐ Medium ☐ Hard ☐

OVERALL RATING ☆☆☆☆☆

NOTES

DESSERTS

Good apple pies are a considerable part of our domestic happiness.

JANE AUSTEN

RECIPE	PAGE

RECIPE

FROM:

SERVINGS:　　　　PREP/COOK TIME:

INGREDIENTS:

NOTES/SUBSTITUTIONS:

DIRECTIONS:

WINE PAIRINGS:

DIFFICULTY:

Easy ☐ Medium ☐ Hard ☐

OVERALL RATING ☆☆☆☆☆

RECIPE

FROM:

SERVINGS: PREP/COOK TIME:

INGREDIENTS:

NOTES/SUBSTITUTIONS:

DIRECTIONS:

WINE PAIRINGS:

DIFFICULTY:

Easy ☐ Medium ☐ Hard ☐

OVERALL RATING ☆☆☆☆☆

RECIPE

FROM:

SERVINGS: PREP/COOK TIME:

INGREDIENTS:

NOTES/SUBSTITUTIONS:

DIRECTIONS:

WINE PAIRINGS:

DIFFICULTY:

Easy ☐ Medium ☐ Hard ☐

OVERALL RATING ☆☆☆☆☆

RECIPE

FROM:

SERVINGS: PREP/COOK TIME:

INGREDIENTS:

NOTES/SUBSTITUTIONS:

DIRECTIONS:

WINE PAIRINGS:

DIFFICULTY:

Easy ☐ Medium ☐ Hard ☐

OVERALL RATING ☆☆☆☆☆

RECIPE

FROM:

SERVINGS: PREP/COOK TIME:

INGREDIENTS:

NOTES/SUBSTITUTIONS:

DIRECTIONS:

WINE PAIRINGS:

DIFFICULTY:

Easy ☐ Medium ☐ Hard ☐

OVERALL RATING ☆☆☆☆☆

RECIPE

FROM:

SERVINGS: PREP/COOK TIME:

INGREDIENTS:

NOTES/SUBSTITUTIONS:

DIRECTIONS:

_____

_____

_____

_____

_____

_____

_____

_____

_____

_____

_____

_____

_____

_____

_____

_____

_____

_____

_____

WINE PAIRINGS:

DIFFICULTY:

Easy ☐ Medium ☐ Hard ☐

OVERALL RATING ☆☆☆☆☆

RECIPE

FROM:

SERVINGS: PREP/COOK TIME:

INGREDIENTS:

NOTES/SUBSTITUTIONS:

DIRECTIONS:

WINE PAIRINGS:

DIFFICULTY:

Easy ☐ Medium ☐ Hard ☐

OVERALL RATING ☆☆☆☆☆

RECEIPE

FROM:

SERVINGS: PREP/COOK TIME:

INGREDIENTS:

NOTES/SUBSTITUTIONS:

DIRECTIONS:

WINE PAIRINGS:

DIFFICULTY:

Easy ☐ Medium ☐ Hard ☐

OVERALL RATING ☆☆☆☆☆

RECIPE

FROM:

SERVINGS: PREP/COOK TIME:

INGREDIENTS:

NOTES/SUBSTITUTIONS:

DIRECTIONS:

WINE PAIRINGS:

DIFFICULTY:

Easy ☐ Medium ☐ Hard ☐

OVERALL RATING ☆☆☆☆☆

RECIPE

FROM:

SERVINGS: PREP/COOK TIME:

INGREDIENTS:

NOTES/SUBSTITUTIONS:

DIRECTIONS:

WINE PAIRINGS:

DIFFICULTY:

Easy ☐ Medium ☐ Hard ☐

OVERALL RATING ☆☆☆☆☆

NOTES

BEVERAGES

The problem with the world is that everyone is a few drinks behind.

HUMPHREY BOGART

RECIPE	PAGE

RECIPE

FROM:

SERVINGS: PREP/COOK TIME:

INGREDIENTS:

NOTES/SUBSTITUTIONS:

DIRECTIONS:

FOOD PAIRINGS:

DIFFICULTY:

Easy ☐ Medium ☐ Hard ☐

OVERALL RATING ☆☆☆☆☆

RECIPE

FROM:

SERVINGS: PREP/COOK TIME:

INGREDIENTS:

NOTES/SUBSTITUTIONS:

DIRECTIONS:

FOOD PAIRINGS:

DIFFICULTY:

Easy ☐ Medium ☐ Hard ☐

OVERALL RATING ☆☆☆☆☆

RECIPE

FROM:

SERVINGS: PREP/COOK TIME:

INGREDIENTS:

NOTES/SUBSTITUTIONS:

DIRECTIONS:

FOOD PAIRINGS:

DIFFICULTY:

Easy ☐ Medium ☐ Hard ☐

OVERALL RATING ☆☆☆☆☆

RECIPE

FROM:

SERVINGS:　　　　PREP/COOK TIME:

INGREDIENTS:

NOTES/SUBSTITUTIONS:

DIRECTIONS:

FOOD PAIRINGS:

DIFFICULTY:

Easy ☐ Medium ☐ Hard ☐

OVERALL RATING ☆☆☆☆☆

RECIPE

FROM:

SERVINGS: PREP/COOK TIME:

INGREDIENTS:

NOTES/SUBSTITUTIONS:

DIRECTIONS:

FOOD PAIRINGS:

DIFFICULTY:

Easy ☐ Medium ☐ Hard ☐

OVERALL RATING ☆☆☆☆☆

RECIPE

FROM:

SERVINGS: PREP/COOK TIME:

INGREDIENTS:

NOTES/SUBSTITUTIONS:

DIRECTIONS:

FOOD PAIRINGS:

DIFFICULTY:

Easy ☐ Medium ☐ Hard ☐

OVERALL RATING ☆☆☆☆☆

RECIPE

FROM:

SERVINGS: PREP/COOK TIME:

INGREDIENTS:

NOTES/SUBSTITUTIONS:

DIRECTIONS:

_____

_____

_____

_____

_____

_____

_____

_____

_____

_____

_____

_____

_____

_____

_____

_____

_____

_____

_____

_____

_____

FOOD PAIRINGS: _____

DIFFICULTY:

Easy ☐ Medium ☐ Hard ☐

OVERALL RATING ☆☆☆☆☆

RECIPE

FROM:

SERVINGS: PREP/COOK TIME:

INGREDIENTS:

NOTES/SUBSTITUTIONS:

DIRECTIONS:

FOOD PAIRINGS:

DIFFICULTY:

Easy ☐ Medium ☐ Hard ☐

OVERALL RATING ☆☆☆☆☆

RECIPE

FROM:

SERVINGS: PREP/COOK TIME:

INGREDIENTS:

NOTES/SUBSTITUTIONS:

DIRECTIONS:

FOOD PAIRINGS:

DIFFICULTY:

Easy ☐ Medium ☐ Hard ☐

OVERALL RATING ☆☆☆☆☆

RECIPE

FROM:

SERVINGS: PREP/COOK TIME:

INGREDIENTS:

NOTES/SUBSTITUTIONS:

DIRECTIONS:

FOOD PAIRINGS:

DIFFICULTY:

Easy ☐ Medium ☐ Hard ☐

OVERALL RATING ☆☆☆☆☆

NOTES

HOLIDAYS & PARTIES

A man hath no better thing under the sun than to eat, and to drink, and to be merry.

ECCLESIASTES 8:15

RECIPE	PAGE

RECIPE

FROM:

SERVINGS: PREP/COOK TIME:

INGREDIENTS:

NOTES/SUBSTITUTIONS:

DIRECTIONS:

WINE PAIRINGS:

DIFFICULTY:

Easy ☐ Medium ☐ Hard ☐

OVERALL RATING ☆☆☆☆☆

RECIPE

FROM:

SERVINGS: PREP/COOK TIME:

INGREDIENTS:

NOTES/SUBSTITUTIONS:

DIRECTIONS:

_____

_____

_____

_____

_____

_____

_____

_____

_____

_____

_____

_____

_____

_____

_____

_____

_____

_____

_____

WINE PAIRINGS:

DIFFICULTY:

Easy ☐ Medium ☐ Hard ☐

OVERALL RATING ☆☆☆☆☆

RECIPE

FROM:

SERVINGS: PREP/COOK TIME:

INGREDIENTS:

NOTES/SUBSTITUTIONS:

DIRECTIONS:

WINE PAIRINGS:

DIFFICULTY:

Easy ☐ Medium ☐ Hard ☐

OVERALL RATING ☆☆☆☆☆

RECIPE

FROM:

SERVINGS:　　　　　PREP/COOK TIME:

INGREDIENTS:

NOTES/SUBSTITUTIONS:

DIRECTIONS:

WINE PAIRINGS:

DIFFICULTY:

Easy ☐ Medium ☐ Hard ☐

OVERALL RATING ☆☆☆☆☆

RECIPE

FROM:

SERVINGS: PREP/COOK TIME:

INGREDIENTS:

NOTES/SUBSTITUTIONS:

DIRECTIONS:

....

....

....

....

....

....

....

....

....

....

....

....

....

....

....

....

....

....

....

....

....

....

WINE PAIRINGS:

DIFFICULTY:

Easy ☐ Medium ☐ Hard ☐

OVERALL RATING ☆☆☆☆☆

RECIPE

FROM:

SERVINGS: PREP/COOK TIME:

INGREDIENTS:

NOTES/SUBSTITUTIONS:

DIRECTIONS:

WINE PAIRINGS:

DIFFICULTY:

Easy ☐ Medium ☐ Hard ☐

OVERALL RATING ☆☆☆☆☆

RECIPE

FROM:

SERVINGS: PREP/COOK TIME:

INGREDIENTS:

NOTES/SUBSTITUTIONS:

DIRECTIONS:

WINE PAIRINGS:

DIFFICULTY:

Easy ☐ Medium ☐ Hard ☐

OVERALL RATING ☆☆☆☆☆

RECIPE

FROM:

SERVINGS: PREP/COOK TIME:

INGREDIENTS:

NOTES/SUBSTITUTIONS:

DIRECTIONS:

....

....

....

....

....

....

....

....

....

....

....

....

....

....

....

....

....

....

....

....

....

WINE PAIRINGS:

DIFFICULTY:

Easy ☐ Medium ☐ Hard ☐

OVERALL RATING ☆☆☆☆☆

RECIPE

FROM:

SERVINGS: PREP/COOK TIME:

INGREDIENTS:

NOTES/SUBSTITUTIONS:

DIRECTIONS:

WINE PAIRINGS:

DIFFICULTY:

Easy ☐ Medium ☐ Hard ☐

OVERALL RATING ☆☆☆☆☆

RECIPE

FROM:

SERVINGS:　　　　PREP/COOK TIME:

INGREDIENTS:

NOTES/SUBSTITUTIONS:

DIRECTIONS:

WINE PAIRINGS:

DIFFICULTY:

Easy ☐ Medium ☐ Hard ☐

OVERALL RATING ☆☆☆☆☆

NOTES

MORE RECIPES

You can tell how long a couple has been married by whether they are on their first, second, or third bottle of Tabasco.

BRUCE BYE

RECIPE	PAGE

RECIPE

FROM:

SERVINGS: PREP/COOK TIME:

INGREDIENTS:

NOTES/SUBSTITUTIONS:

DIRECTIONS:

WINE PAIRINGS:

DIFFICULTY:

Easy ☐ Medium ☐ Hard ☐

OVERALL RATING ☆☆☆☆☆

RECIPE

FROM:

SERVINGS: | PREP/COOK TIME:

INGREDIENTS:

NOTES/SUBSTITUTIONS:

DIRECTIONS:

WINE PAIRINGS:

DIFFICULTY:

Easy ☐ Medium ☐ Hard ☐

OVERALL RATING ☆☆☆☆☆

RECIPE

FROM:

SERVINGS: PREP/COOK TIME:

INGREDIENTS:

NOTES/SUBSTITUTIONS:

DIRECTIONS:

WINE PAIRINGS:

DIFFICULTY:

Easy ☐ Medium ☐ Hard ☐

OVERALL RATING ☆☆☆☆☆

RECIPE

FROM:

SERVINGS: PREP/COOK TIME:

INGREDIENTS:

NOTES/SUBSTITUTIONS:

DIRECTIONS:

WINE PAIRINGS:

DIFFICULTY:

Easy ☐ Medium ☐ Hard ☐

OVERALL RATING ☆☆☆☆☆

RECIPE

FROM:

SERVINGS: PREP/COOK TIME:

INGREDIENTS:

NOTES/SUBSTITUTIONS:

DIRECTIONS:

WINE PAIRINGS:

DIFFICULTY:

Easy ☐ Medium ☐ Hard ☐

OVERALL RATING ☆☆☆☆☆

RECIPE

FROM:

SERVINGS: PREP/COOK TIME:

INGREDIENTS:

NOTES/SUBSTITUTIONS:

DIRECTIONS:

WINE PAIRINGS:

DIFFICULTY:

Easy ☐ Medium ☐ Hard ☐

OVERALL RATING ☆☆☆☆☆

RECIPE

FROM:

SERVINGS: PREP/COOK TIME:

INGREDIENTS:

NOTES/SUBSTITUTIONS:

DIRECTIONS:

WINE PAIRINGS:

DIFFICULTY:

Easy ☐ Medium ☐ Hard ☐

OVERALL RATING ☆☆☆☆☆

RECIPE

FROM:

SERVINGS: PREP/COOK TIME:

INGREDIENTS:

NOTES/SUBSTITUTIONS:

DIRECTIONS:

WINE PAIRINGS:

DIFFICULTY:

Easy ☐ Medium ☐ Hard ☐

OVERALL RATING ☆☆☆☆☆

RECEIPE

FROM:

SERVINGS: PREP/COOK TIME:

INGREDIENTS:

NOTES/SUBSTITUTIONS:

DIRECTIONS:

WINE PAIRINGS:

DIFFICULTY:

Easy ☐ Medium ☐ Hard ☐

OVERALL RATING ☆☆☆☆☆

RECIPE

FROM:

SERVINGS: PREP/COOK TIME:

INGREDIENTS:

NOTES/SUBSTITUTIONS:

DIRECTIONS:

_____
_____
_____
_____
_____
_____
_____
_____
_____
_____
_____
_____
_____
_____
_____
_____
_____
_____
_____
_____
_____
_____
_____
_____

WINE PAIRINGS: _____

DIFFICULTY:

Easy ☐ Medium ☐ Hard ☐

OVERALL RATING ☆☆☆☆☆

NOTES

FOOD FOR THOUGHT

Poets have been mysteriously silent on the subject of cheese.

G. K. CHESTERTON

FAVORITE COOKING PROGRAMS, PUBLICATIONS, & WEB SITES

NAME   NOTES:

SELECTED RECIPES FROM
FAVORITE COOKBOOKS

RECIPE	COOKBOOK	PAGE

SELECTED RECIPES FROM
FAVORITE COOKBOOKS

RECIPE	COOKBOOK	PAGE